Making Each
Moment Count

Anne Bryan Smollin

Making Each Moment Count

21 Reflections on a Fulfilled Life

NEW CITY PRESS
Hyde Park, NY

Published in the United States by New City Press
202 Comforter Blvd., Hyde Park, NY 12538
www.newcitypress.com
©2011 Anne Bryan Smollin

Cover design by Leandro de Leon

Library of Congress Cataloging-in-Publication Data:

Smollin, Anne Bryan.
  Making each moment count : 21 reflections on a fulfilled life / Anne Bryan Smollin.
    p. cm.
  ISBN 978-1-56548-367-5 (pbk. : alk. paper) 1. Self-realization—Religious aspects—Christianity—
Meditations. I. Title.
  BV4598.2.S56 2011
  242—dc22   2010044531

Printed in the United States of America

Contents

Introduction

*W*hat a privilege I feel in being able to share these thoughts with you. I envision this little book as a "thought for the day," and so we can spend 21 days together. Some psychologists claim that it takes 21 days to change a habit or establish a behavior. Isn't it worth 21 days effort to become more grounded in the moment and capable of living fully and enjoying life with others and with God?

I have also included some of my own photos of flowers. Everyone needs a hobby; mine is photography. These flowers have inspired my prayer and brought beauty into my life. I hope that they inspire you to find your own unique and personal ways to nurture beauty in your daily life. Our senses grow stronger when we cultivate an awareness of beauty: smelling the sweet fragrance of a flower, noticing how each petal unfolds and complements the other, or even touching the gentle smoothness of a leaf.

I hope that this small book will help you to discover who you truly are and foster an awareness of all the blessings that surround you. Within the ordinariness of daily life may you find graces clothed in the surprise and wonder of the beauty and blessings around you.

Be in the Moment

$\mathscr{S}$tress, pressures, demands from others, deadlines, and negative moments fill many days. Slowing down to enter the present is a challenge. Our minds wander. We worry about what needs to be done and even about what we have done.

"If only," or "Why didn't I?" or "Maybe I could" clutter our minds and mask our peace.

The present moment is the only reality we have. This very second contains everything needed to live life fully and positively. Holding on to negative thoughts clogs the brain and leaves us stuck. Not living in the present saps our energy and distracts us from joy and creativity.

Today let us "seize the moment." Consider the people on the *Titanic* that passed up dessert!

This very moment has all the grace and joy we need to live fully.

❧

Celebrate Your Reflection

*O*ften, we forget to celebrate the person we see in the mirror. We tend to downplay who we are and the gifts with which we have been endowed. God has blessed us and graced our lives with unique and wonderful gifts. How do we make ourselves aware of our gifts and talents and then acknowledge them? By acknowledging these God-given blessings, we express our gratitude for God's generosity in our lives and glorify God's name by sharing who we are and what we have.

"You are the light of the world. A city built on a hill cannot be hid. No one after lighting a lamp puts it under the bushel basket, but on the lampstand, and it gives light to all in the house. In the same way, let your light shine before others, so that they may see your good works and give glory to your Father in heaven" (Mt 5:15–16).

Doing something for another — a simple act like helping an elderly person cross the street or holding a door open for another — gives your immune system a boost. Even more enlightening is the fact that a person who merely witnesses such kind deeds will also get a boost.

Not only do we stay healthier and happier using our gifts for others, but we also enrich other people because of our actions.

"You received without payment; give without payment" (Mt 10:8).

See the Obvious

We **of**ten miss the obvious, the blessings right in front of us. We miss the smile that communicates another's happiness at seeing us; a kind word or note that conveys another's need for us. We take for granted the beauty of a sunrise or a sunset, the loveliness of a flowering meadow. Too often we deny our souls nourishment by missing the obvious.

A beggar had been sitting by the side of a road for over 30 years. As the story goes, one day a stranger walked by. "Spare some change?" mumbled the beggar, mechanically holding out his old baseball cap.

"I have nothing to give you," said the stranger. Then he asked: "What's that you are sitting on?"

"Nothing," replied the beggar. "Just an old box. I have been sitting on it for as long as I can remember."

"Ever looked inside?" asked the stranger.

"No," said the beggar. "What's the point? There's nothing in there."

"Take a look inside," insisted the stranger.

The beggar managed to pry open the lid. With astonishment, disbelief, and elation, he saw that the box was filled with gold.

Give yourself the obvious, the treasures found in the present moment. Stop and smell the roses! Look into the eyes of the one who blesses you with a smile; listen with new ears to what a friend is really sharing with you. Daily moments hold hidden treasures and untold blessings.

Choose Happiness
and Laugh Often

*H*appiness is a choice. Some people we know choose not to be happy. They see the negative in everything. Nothing is ever right — they never get the recognition they deserve; every picnic they plan gets rained out; every good idea they have is stolen by somebody else. You know them. They complain often and even seem to relish hearing themselves complain.

Living in the moment and finding joy in the present empowers a person to choose happiness. Joy is an attitude that maintains health. It frees the brain and expands the heart. Of all self-talk (the monologue we carry on in our heads) 80% is negative; 75% of all conversation is negative. Negative energy smothers joy and happiness. Negativity makes us feel uncomfortable and drains our energy. We need to make a conscious choice to be positive. Putting some laughter in our day will open our awareness to the positive energy around us.

A French proverb advises, "The most completely lost of all days is the one in which we have not laughed." Laughter is medicine for the soul. It improves everything — from imagination to creativity, relationships to circulation. Laughter suspends worries and problems and helps us feel better.

Laughter relaxes the muscles. It makes us feel safer and more secure. Laughter helps strengthen social bonds; we grow closer to others and deepen trust. Laughter broadens our vision and sustains our hope. It empowers us to see and believe that things can change for the better. Laughter doesn't eliminate pain and anxiety; it allows us to handle such feelings. Laughter helps us to see potential and to consider possibility.

People who help us laugh are a gift to us. Alternately, we bestow blessings on others when we help them laugh. Let this be a day to grace another's life with the gift of laughter and choose happiness.

Welcome All

The Letter to the Hebrews contains this beautiful quotation: "Do not neglect to show hospitality to strangers, for by doing that some have entertained angels without knowing it" (Heb 13:2).

Today, treat everyone like an angel: share a smile with all you meet — friend or stranger; acknowledge others by making eye contact; give the gift of recognition by greeting passersby with a glance; welcome family and friends with a hug or a friendly word. Such simple gestures convey the dignity and respect they deserve.

Sharing life moments with another opens our own hearts and enriches our lives. These casual encounters help us grow. We share dreams and stories, hopes and fears. We find the sacrament of daily life; we become communion with and for the other.

An Irish proverb sums it up: "It is in the shelter of each other that the people live."

❧

Accept what Is

$\mathcal{S}$ometimes we need to learn to be content with what *is* and what we have. We wish things were different; we "want" or "need" more things. We wish we were someplace else, with someone else. Nothing ever seems quite right; something always seems missing or lacking. Peace comes when we accept whatever *is* in the moment and avoid wasting energy on what *is not*.

The experience of Nasrudin, the wise fool, demonstrates how to find contentment in what *is*. Nasrudin decided to start a flower garden. He prepared the soil and planted the seeds. As they grew, lovely flowers bloomed, but so did dandelions. He sought advice near and far; he tried every method gardeners suggested to eliminate the pesky weeds, all to no avail. Finally he went to the palace to seek advice from the wise old royal gardener. Every remedy he proposed, Nasrudin had already tried. They sat in silence for some time. Finally the gardener looked at Nasrudin and said, "Well then, I suggest you learn to love dandelions."

When you find yourself frustrated or anxious today, take a deep breath and whisper a prayer for acceptance. What you can't change, decide to accept.

You Decide

*T*oday has just begun. You have no idea what will transpire or what experiences you will record at its end. You may meet up with someone lonely, someone who feels abandoned or rejected. Your smile may be the only warmth that person experiences today. Perhaps acknowledging an old man with a greeting will give him the grace to go on. Maybe it will be a confused adolescent, isolated from her peer group and lacking a sense of belonging. Perhaps your warmth will bring comfort and security to a frightened and fearful child.

In each of these scenarios the difference is YOU. Because YOU were not so rushed, you noticed; because YOU were not absorbed in your own world, they felt acknowledged and valued.

Consider the story of a young rabbi who came to a town seeking followers. A renowned rabbi there, however, already had the townspeople's respect and honor. The frustrated young rabbi concocted a plan: he would approach the elder rabbi with a bird in his hand and ask if the bird is dead or alive. If the old rabbi says the bird is dead, he will open his hand and let the bird fly away. But if the old rabbi says the bird is alive he will crush it. Either way he hoped to embarrass his rival so as to lure away his followers.

"Tell me Rabbi," the young one asked, "is this bird dead or alive?"

The old rabbi looked at the inexperienced young man and said, "Really my friend, it's up to you!"

So, too, is this day "up to YOU." Greet someone; acknowledge another's presence; grace that person's day with a smile. Will YOU make a difference? "Really my friend, it's up to you."

Caress the Butterfly

We are busy. We leave no free moments and no uncluttered space. We surround ourselves with stimuli — televisions, iPods, cell phones, computers, music — and not enough quiet. Multitasking is considered a virtue, while focused attention and single-mindedness have all but disappeared from our vocabulary.

Silence teaches us so much. We hear the summer breeze blow through trees and we listen to the peaceful silence of a winter snowfall. We hear ourselves and we listen to God.

When we program all of our lives, we miss the imperceptible fall of snowflakes, the rushing of the trees, or the chirping of a bird. We deny ourselves the beauty of a flower, the warmth of the sun on our face, the joy of a simple smile.

Perhaps today we can slow ourselves down. Slow down to seize the moment of silence, to live the present, to notice what is before us. God speaks in silence, through nature, between encounters. For our part, we have to listen.

Here is a story about the many ways God is revealed:

The man whispered, "God, speak to me."
And the meadowlark sang.
But the man did not hear.
So the man yelled, "God, speak to me."
And thunder and lightning rolled across the sky.
But the man did not listen.
The man looked around and said, "God, let me see you."
And a star shone.
But the man did not see.
And the man shouted, "God, show me a miracle."
And a life was born.
But the man did not notice.
So the man cried out in despair, "Touch me, God,
and let me know you are here."
Whereupon God reached down and touched the man.
But the man brushed the butterfly away and walked on.

Let us open our ears to wonder and our eyes to surprise, consciously slowing down so as to receive what God offers in the moment.

❧

Offer Gratitude

"It's going to be a long day." "I have so much to do."
"There is no one I can depend on."
"I'm so tired and the day hasn't begun."

These statements reveal the kind of day you will have. It will be a day so filled with negativity that it becomes a self-fulfilling prophecy: nothing good can happen.

Take a deep breath and begin the day again. Think how blessed you are with another day; thank God that you showed up again! Think of three things for which you are grateful. Perhaps you enjoy good health or are in a good relationship. Maybe you have a secure home and food on your table. Perhaps you have no debt or your children are all happy, living productive, satisfying lives. Create your own list of gratitude; see how many you can add as you reflect on these blessings throughout the day.

Be thankful for the cool breeze on a hot summer day or the scent of spring after an April rain. Be grateful for the eyesight that lets you take in a sunrise, read a book, or glimpse a hummingbird. Be grateful for the sense of hearing that allows you to enter into beautiful music, hear kind words, or imitate a cricket's song.

Gratitude is an attitude. We determine our own attitudes, how we want to be. We cannot control events but we can control our response. The more we develop an attitude of gratitude the more we develop an awareness of our blessings. Living gratitude enables us to balance life's daily stresses; it empowers us to live from abundance and strength. We begin to see our life over-flowing with goodness and joy.

So let today be a day of gratitude, celebrating all that is in each and every event and person we encounter.

Set Yourself Free

When we carry old hurts and hold deep anger, we build walls of isolation and block moments of grace. People hold on to hurtful spoken words for years. Some foster alienation, choosing not to speak to another person because of something that occurred between them.

When we hold on to negative memories we are hurting only ourselves. We let the hurt or anger eat away at us. We rehearse the words that were spoken over and over again in our heads, as if carving them into our very muscles. We are not willing to forget.

Consider this story of two men who had been imprisoned together. For years they were constantly abused and beaten, but finally were released. Years later the two encountered each other. Overjoyed at seeing one another again, they embraced. One turned to the other and asked, "Tell me, have you forgiven them for all they did to us?"

The other quickly responded, "No. I cannot forgive what they did to us. All the abuse and torture. No, never."

The first responded, "So, they still have you in prison."

That's what happens when we hold on to old hurts. We imprison ourselves.

Let Go of Judgment

*H*ow often we let another's actions disturb us. We make judgments and write monologues in our minds condemning their behavior. We recall something said or done months after it happened. We keep the incident alive, rehearsing it and remembering our self-composed verdict while reveling in self-righteousness.

There once were two monks on a journey, walking silently over hills and past forests, absorbed in the beauty of the countryside. They came to a stream, where they noticed a woman standing at the bank. The water was shallow, but it was wide and swift.

One of the monks went over, picked her up and carried her to the other side. He set her down on solid ground and re-crossed the stream to join his companion.

After a mile the other broke the silence. "I can't believe what you just did. We are celibate men. We are not even supposed to touch a woman, much less carry one across a stream."

The other responded, "I put her down a mile back. You're still carrying her in your mind."

Why do we insist on carrying such baggage?

Today let us gift self and others with compassion, letting go of judgmental attitudes and self-righteous behavior.

Lighten Your Load

$\mathscr{D}$id you ever laugh so hard that your sides hurt and tears rolled down your cheeks? Sometimes it's even hard to catch your breath when laughing that hard. At such moments, we are fully alive. Absorbed in the present, not a moment of the past owns us nor does a moment of worry or concern for the future consume us.

The gift of laughter offers multiple benefits. It is one of the best physical exercises. Body temperature rises at least one degree. The glottis and larynx begin to rock. Air rumbles up along the windpipe, banging against the trachea and exploding out of our bodies at 70 miles per hour!

Laughter has a spiritual connection. We feel a closer bond to people with whom we laugh. We trust them more. When we laugh with others we give each other hope and confidence; we believe we can make it through a difficult situation.

It doesn't change anything permanently. It does, however, make us take deep breaths and sends oxygen to the brain. It might even give us a new perspective.

Laughter helps us take ourselves more lightly. Best yet, it is flexible: we can laugh with one person, in a crowd, or alone.

Today can be your laughter day. Laugh when you see something funny or silly. Laugh when you can't find your glasses or keys. Laugh when you make a mistake. Laugh when someone shares a funny incident. Laugh with a child or an elderly person. Blessed with this healthy prescription, you will feel better at the end of the day.

Victor Hugo said, "Laughter is the sun that drives winter from the human face."

Laughter is medicine for the soul.

Enjoy the Day

*T*ake time to enjoy the day! We are in such a rush. People and events detain us, frustrate us, and anger us — stoplights, yield signs, slow drivers, enraged drivers, detours, traffic; fast people, slow people, late people, early people, young people, old people; and everything in-between or in our way. We don't even enjoy food and meal times together because we feel like we need to be somewhere else with someone else. Health obsession and perfect-body-syndrome has shifted our attention from savoring the food and sharing the company to counting the grams and measuring the cholesterol.

So many outside forces steal our happiness. Buddha taught, "With our thoughts we make our world. Think evil thoughts and as surely as the cart follows the ox, evil will follow you. Think good thoughts, and goodness will surely be yours."

The day is shaped by our thoughts. We can arrive late to an appointment and be angry, frustrated, and anxious, or we can arrive at an appointment late.

We create the world around us. Today let us listen to our thoughts and be aware of our own inner compass. What will drive us: calm and peace, or anxiety and frustration?

Rumi's simple poem challenges us to be grounded in the moment and to make a difference. "Be a light, a ladder, a lifeboat. Help someone's soul heal."

Be Yourself

There is only one YOU. No one else has the same DNA or fingerprints. No one else has the same number of hairs as you have on your head or the same pattern of wrinkles as the ones when you smile.

We only need to be ourselves. So often we want to be like another person. We try to imitate their way of being, manner of speech, or style of hair. We may aspire to be like some famous athlete, movie star, or musician. The true gift is the uniqueness of our self, the person we are, complete with our own strengths and foibles. We need only to become the person we really are. A holy rabbi once told his disciples, "When I get to heaven God isn't going to ask me, 'Rabbi Yosef, why weren't you more like Moses?' No, God will ask me, 'Rabbi Yosef, why weren't you more like the Yosef whom I created?'"

So I should make today a day where I grow more comfortable and confident with ME, with the person I am. I should recognize my gifts and talents and take responsibility for using them. I can make the world a better place today because of my presence in it. I should grow into my potential, being the gift that God created and becoming all that God imagined of me.

Today let us accept who we are, acknowledging our gifts and limitations. If we cannot plant a garden, let us delight in the beauty of another's. If we cannot bake our own bread, let us celebrate another's culinary skills when we break bread together. Let us offer our uniqueness as gift and celebrate the distinctiveness of others. Complementing each other, we serve a world in need. The gift we share is the person we are. We bring to each moment of our day "me." As we grace the world with our presence, we find we have been richly blessed by the other.

✼

Dream Dreams

I went to the hospital to visit a friend who was dying. She had been diagnosed with cancer and knew she had little time left on her earthly journey. She said, "Anne, be careful what you pray for." Her husband had died suddenly, leaving her with two small children. She asked God to keep her healthy so she could raise her children and provide for their well-being. She felt it was her responsibility to take care of them until they married, so she prayed, "God, let me have my health so I can see them graduate from college and get married."

As I sat next to her bed in the hospital room, she told me her youngest son had just gotten married two months ago. Her eldest daughter was pregnant. Almost as soon as she had fulfilled her responsibilities, she received her diagnosis. Oscar Wilde wrote, "In this world there are two tragedies. One is not getting what one wants and the other is getting it. The last is much the worst."

But we must dream and hope. We must live with anticipation of what life can offer and what might come. Life is an adventure, not a destination. When I taught first grade, it was important that the children felt free to color, even if they went outside the lines. If learning meant staying inside the lines, what a boring and dull model I would be fostering.

It is for us to color outside the lines. It is for us to be open in prayer to ask for what we need and to dream of what might be. Life is not planned or rational. John Lennon said, "Life is what happens while you are making other plans." God took care of us in the past and will care for us in the future.

According to Grandma Moses, "Life is what we make it. Always has been; always will be." And what we pray for tells us what we value and what is important to us. Let us dream dreams and listen to silent prayers.

Break Bread Together

We weren't created to be alone. We need others. Our companions help us know who we truly are and encourage us to become all that we might be. The word "companion" comes from the Latin *com*, meaning "with," and *panis*, meaning "bread." It literally means "one who breaks bread with another."

Adam wasn't happy alone. He had everything: food, freedom, no pressures, time to do whatever he wanted. In wisdom, however, God saw that, "It is not good that the man should be alone," and so created "a helper as his partner." Eve became the first companion.

When he began his public ministry, Jesus immediately chose companions. Whenever he faced a difficult problem, he would surround himself with his companions. He didn't do it alone.

We, too, need support. We need to connect with others and walk with them on our journey. We must share life and love if we want to grow in (w)holiness. Perhaps it is a reminder:

being made in God's image, we must grow into God's likeness as relational people, becoming bread for and with others.

Live Life Fully

*W*hy do we so fear being "human"? That's how we were created. As human beings we think, imagine, feel, and create. We touch and are touched by graced moments in each day. To see how a complete human being acts and feels, we only have to look at Jesus. He gave bread to the hungry and cried when his friend died. He embraced little children and forgave those who betrayed him. He spent time eating and drinking with his friends. He went to weddings; he reached out to console his friends when they needed it. He taught and he challenged. And he spent time alone.

To be truly human means to be fully alive, to seize the life and possibility of each moment, reaching out and connecting with those who need our presence. It means feeding the hungry, visiting the imprisoned and lonely, attending to the sick, and clothing the naked. The Chinese have a saying, "When someone shares with you something of value, you have an obligation to share it with others." Why wait to do good? We must not be passive, but proactive. We must engage in life, initiating and co-creating. We must *make* our world into the place that God imagines for us.

Share Kindness

Sometimes it is easier to love than to be kind. We can love people close to us or those far away, even hundreds of miles from us. But to be kind means to be selfless enough to act in the moment. It means helping the person in need right here and now. It means getting up to serve someone a cup of coffee or consciously setting aside a current activity to help carry in the groceries. It means being gracious, choosing to perform acts of loving kindness and attending to others' needs.

In these precious acts, giver and receiver share the blessing. Acts of kindness focus on the needs of others and communicate care for the other. It makes those who are close feel loved and valued.

A smile is a gesture of kindness. William Arthur Ward states, "A warm smile is the universal language of kindness." The simple act of opening a door or just saying "Hi" communicates kindness.

Mother Teresa encourages, "Spread your love everywhere you go. First of all in your own house. Give love to your children, to your wife and husband, to a next-door neighbor … let no one ever come to you without leaving better and happier. Be the living expression of God's kindness; kindness in your face, kindness in your eyes, kindness in your smile, kindness in your warm greeting."

"Kindness in words creates confidence; kindness in thinking creates profoundness; kindness in giving creates love" (Lao-Tse).

Be Compassionate

Although it cannot be substantiated definitively, one story has been repeated that reveals Fiorello H. La Guardia's compassion. One cold night in 1935 he entered a courtroom in a poor neighborhood, dismissed the judge for the evening, and took the bench.

La Guardia's first case involved an old woman who had been arrested for theft. When asked to enter her plea she replied, "I needed the bread, Your Honor, to feed my grandchildren."

"I've got to punish you," the mayor responded. The law makes no exceptions. Ten dollars or ten days in jail."

As he pronounced the sentence, he threw $10.00 into his hat. "Here is the ten dollar fine which I now remit; and furthermore I am going to fine everyone in this courtroom 50 cents for living in a town where a person has to steal food so her grandchildren can eat. Mr. Bailiff, collect the fines and give them to the defendant." The woman left the courtroom with $47.50.

Caring enough about others to see what they need and opening our hearts to help them is true compassion. Today we may stand behind a garrulous old man in the supermarket check-out line, or wait at a stop light next to an exasperated driver with fussy children in car seats, or hear a sad and discouraged school child return home. A compassionate response might be a listening ear, a gracious smile or a whispered prayer.

Expect Surprises

*W*hat surprises are waiting for me today? What graces will come my way? Who will carry the message? What will it be and how will it be packaged? Will I recognize it as gift?

Instead of deciding what my day will be like and what needs to happen, let me live these next 24 hours with abandon, open to the possibilities that dangle before me.

The message may come in a conversation. Perhaps it will be in a piece of music. A billboard message may touch me or a card I receive in the mail may catch me off guard. The messenger may be a friend, a family member, even a stranger. I hope I manage to fling my heart open wide to receive it. I hope I am not so busy doing whatever I'm doing that I miss that surprise!

Pause today. Stop on the hour and take a deep breath. Take a moment to look around; notice your surroundings. Become a student of life and allow these moments to teach you. Discover the lesson hidden in each moment.

Night after night, a man was agitated by a recurring dream. Each morning he awoke with a piercing headache, absolutely exhausted. Finally he went to a psychiatrist.

The doctor asked him to repeat the dream. "Each night, I am trying to open a large glass door with a single word printed on it. I must go through. All night long I pull and pull, but the door will not open. At the end of my dream I am so exhausted that I just collapse at the bottom of that door."

The psychiatrist asked, "What word is printed on the door?" The man answered, "Push."

Such surprises may provide an insight, an occasion to learn something new, or a message that brings a smile to your face. Take these moments as life's gift. Let them challenge you to live with openness and excitement on the edge of possibility.

Be Child-like

$\mathcal{O}$ne of my greatest privileges is to become "Santa" for the holiday entertainment. I come down the corridor booming "Ho, ho, ho. Merry Christmas" in the deepest voice I can manage. I repeat it over and over. The faces of the little children fill with wonder as Santa appears. Their eyes light up and they beam with delight. They run up and hug me and hold on tightly. They want to sit on my lap and have their picture taken with me. Their sheer joy is magical!

How much children can teach us! Their open minds and innocent spirit let fantasy and creativity flourish. They trust. They believe and want to believe. They take my hand and dance with me; they do anything I do and follow where I go. They love this jolly old Santa whose splendid, magical presence is more important than any present.

Undaunted by this big person with a white beard and wearing a singular red suit, they are not afraid to ask questions. They nourish their curiosity. One little girl asked, "Santa, where are your reindeers?" I responded, "They are outside waiting for me. I'm sorry I can't stay long. I need to get back to the North Pole. I have a lot to do to get everything ready for Christmas." She ran over to the window, pressed her face hard against the pane, and let out a scream, "I see them!" Five deer just happened to be grazing at that moment on the hillside. All the other children ran to see them. (Tell me God doesn't have a sense of humor!)

Child-like: open, curious, undaunted; trusting, loving, innocent. Today, be child-like. Be light-hearted and dance. Give your heart a chance to linger in the delight of playful moments.